D0338128

KANTO HANDBOOK

by Katherine Noll
and Tracey West

SCHOLASTIC INC.
New York Toronto London Auckland Sydney
Mexico City New Delhi Hong Kong Buenos Aires

Thanks to Karim and Aziz, for all of their help.
And a big thanks to Lauren, too!

No part of this publication may be reproduced in whole or in part, or stored in a retrieval system, or transmitted in any form or by any means, electronic, mechanical, photocopying, recording, or otherwise, without written permission of the publisher. For information regarding permission, write to Scholastic Inc., Attention: Permissions Department, 557 Broadway, New York, NY 10012.

ISBN 0-439-74146-7

© 2005 Pokémon. © 1995-2005 Nintendo/Creatures Inc./GAME FREAK inc. ™ and ® are trademarks of Nintendo. All rights reserved.
Published by Scholastic Inc.
SCHOLASTIC and associated logos are trademarks and/or registered trademarks of Scholastic Inc.

12 11 10 9 8 7 6 5 4 3 2 1 5 6 7 8 9/0

Printed in the U.S.A.
First printing, February 2005

CALLING ALL POKéMON TRAINERS!

So you think you've got everything you need to start your Pokémon journey, right? Empty Poké Balls waiting to be filled. A handy Pokédex packed with facts. It's a good start. But there's just one more thing you need to do . . .

READ THIS HANDBOOK!

That's right. Because things have changed. And the only way to get the scoop on what's been happening is to check out the pages of this guide. Here's what you'll find inside this Official Kanto Handbook:

- Pictures, facts, and stats for 190 Kanto Pokémon! That's the most Pokémon in any Official Handbook so far!

- The lowdown on a whole new addition to the World of Pokémon.

This is stuff you **NEED** to know! So turn the page, kick up your feet, and start reading. You'll be glad you did!

WHAT'S NEW

Forget everything you think you know about Pokémon. Things have really gotten stirred up in the Kanto Region, where Ash started his Pokémon journey. There is new equipment, new ways to battle, and even new islands to explore! Here are some things to look for before you begin your quest:

New Choices

Good news for fans of Misty and May! In your Kanto journey, you can start out your Pokémon as either a boy or a girl Trainer.

New Gear

Professor Oak—provides you your Pokédex. Every Pokémon Trainer needs a Pokédex, a handheld computer that contains stats and info about all kinds of Pokémon. Well, now your Handbook is even better! It's easier to search for what you're looking for, has lots more information, and great portraits to boot!

As a Pokémon Trainer, you'll meet a lot of people on your journey, and many of them will have important things to tell you. But what if you can't remember? With your new Voice Checker, you view what the person said to you—quickly and easily.

Better Battles

In a typical battle, you and your opponent battle by choosing one Pokémon at a time. But now the custom popular in Hoenn is making it's way to the Kanto region—2-on-2 battles! That's double the action!

WHO'S THAT POKéMON?

There are so many Pokémon to catch in the Kanto region! How will you keep track of them all? On the following pages, you'll find pictures and facts about the Pokémon you will encounter. Here are some tips to help you get the 411 you need:

Use the Index:

On page 80, you'll find an index of Pokémon in alphabetical order. If you're looking for a specific Pokémon, look up its name in the index. Then go to the page number listed to find out more about it.

Be Aware of Evolutions:

Some Pokémon have the ability to change into brand-new Pokémon. In this book, we've grouped together Pokémon related by Evolution. Look for these arrows ▼ for a quick look at a Pokémon's evolutionary chain. Or read the stats to find out exactly how a Pokémon evolves.

Keep an eye out for extra tips to help you become a better Pokémon Trainer!

Ready to go? Turn the page to begin your Pokémon journey. Just don't forget your Poké Balls!

BULBASAUR *Seed Pokémon*

Type: Grass/Poison
How to say it: BUL-buh-sore
Height: 2' 4"
Weight: 15 lbs
Possible Moves: Tackle, Growl, Leech Seed, Vine Whip, Poison-powder, Razor Leaf, Sweet Scent, Growth, Sleep Powder, Synthesis, Solarbeam
Evolves: into Ivysaur

IVYSAUR *Seed Pokémon*

Type: Grass/Poison
How to say it: EYE-vee-sore
Height: 3' 3"
Weight: 29 lbs
Possible Moves: Tackle, Growl, Leech Seed, Vine Whip, Poison-powder, Razor Leaf, Sweet Scent, Growth, Sleep Powder, Solarbeam
Evolves: into Venusaur

VENUSAUR *Seed Pokémon*

Type: Grass/Poison
How to say it: VEE-nuh-sore
Height: 6' 7"
Weight: 221 lbs
Possible Moves: Tackle, Growl, Leech Seed, Vine Whip, Poison-powder, Razor Leaf, Sweet Scent, Growth, Sleep Powder, Synthesis, Solarbeam
Does not evolve

The bulb on Bulbasaur's back is used to store energy. The bulb gets bigger when Bulbasaur evolves into Ivysaur. When Ivysaur becomes Venusaur, the bulb blooms into a huge flower. The flower collects sunlight to power Venusaur's attacks!

Keep an eye on Charmander's tail! When the little Fire Pokémon is angry, the flame burns brightly. But if the flame goes out, Charmander could be in big trouble! Of course, by the time Charmander evolves into Charizard, its flames are so super hot they can melt boulders!

CHARMANDER *Lizard Pokémon*

Type: Fire
How to say it: CHAR-man-der
Height: 2' 0"
Weight: 19 lbs
Possible Moves: Scratch, Growl, Ember, Metal Claw, Smokescreen, Scary Face, Slash, Flamethrower, Dragon Rage, Fire Spin
Evolves: into Charmeleon

CHARMELEON *Lizard Pokémon*

Type: Fire
How to say it: char-MEAL-ee-ehn
Height: 3' 7"
Weight: 42 lbs
Possible Moves: Scratch, Growl, Ember, Metal Claw, Smokescreen, Scary Face, Slash, Flamethrower, Dragon Rage, Fire Spin
Evolves: into Charizard

CHARIZARD *Flame Pokémon*

Type: Fire/Flying
How to say it: CHAR-i-zard
Height: 5' 7"
Weight: 200 lbs
Possible Moves: Heat Wave, Scratch, Growl, Ember, Metal Claw, Smokescreen, Scary Face, Slash, Flamethrower, Wing Attack, Dragon Rage, Fire Spin
Does not evolve

SQUIRTLE *Tiny Turtle Pokémon*

Type: Water
How to say it: SKWIR-tuhl
Height: 1' 8"
Weight: 20 lbs
Possible Moves: Tackle, Tail Whip, Bubble, Water Gun, Bite, Rapid Spin, Protect, Rain Dance, Withdraw, Skull Bash, Hydro Pump
Evolves: into Wartortle

WARTORTLE *Turtle Pokémon*

Type: Water
Pronunciation: WAR-tor-tuhl
Height: 3' 3"
Weight: 50 lbs
Possible Moves: Tackle, Tail Whip, Bubble, Water Gun, Bite, Rapid Spin, Protect, Rain Dance, Withdraw, Skull Bash, Hydro Pump
Evolves: into Blastoise

BLASTOISE *Shellfish Pokémon*

Type: Water
How to say it: BLAS-toys
Height: 5' 3"
Weight: 189 lbs
Possible Moves: Tackle, Tail Whip, Bubble, Water Gun, Bite, Rapid Spin, Protect, Rain Dance, Withdraw, Skull Bash, Hydro Pump
Does not evolve

Squirtle is cute, but tough. Its hard shell protects it from attacks. If you look, you can see scratches on Wartortle's shell from all of its battles. But Blastoise might have the best shell of all. Big cannons protrude from it, ready to blast opponents with Water Attacks!

Caterpie likes to munch on leaves all day so it can store up its energy for when it evolves into Metapod. Metapod stays inside its shell without moving. It does not leave its shell until it has evolved into the flying Butterfree.

CATERPIE *Worm Pokémon*

Type: Bug
How to say it: CAT-er-pee
Height: 1' 0"
Weight: 6 lbs
Possible Moves: Tackle, String Shot
Evolves: into Metapod

METAPOD *Cocoon Pokémon*

Type: Bug
How to say it: MET-uh-pod
Height: 2' 4"
Weight: 22 lbs
Possible Moves: Harden
Evolves: into Butterfree

BUTTERFREE *Butterfly Pokémon*

Type: Bug/Flying
How to say it: BUT-er-free
Height: 3' 7"
Weight: 71 lbs
Possible Moves: Confusion, Poisonpowder, Stun Spore, Sleep Powder, Supersonic, Whirlwind, Gust, Psybeam, Safeguard, Silver Wind
Does not evolve

WEEDLE

Hairy Bug Pokémon

Type: Bug/Poison
How to say it: WEE-dull
Height: 1' 0"
Weight: 7 lbs
Possible Moves: Poison Sting, String Shot
Evolves: into Kakuna

KAKUNA

Cocoon Pokémon

Type: Bug/Poison
How to say it: ka-KOO-nuh
Height: 2' 0"
Weight: 22 lbs
Possible Moves: Harden
Evolves: into Beedrill

BEEDRILL

Poison Bee Pokémon

Type: Bug/Poison
How to say it: BEE-drill
Height: 3' 3"
Weight: 65 lbs
Possible Moves: Fury Attack, Focus Energy, Twineedle, Rage, Pursuit, Pin Missile, Agility, Endeavor
Does not evolve

The stinger on top of Weedle's head is poisonous. Weedle keeps its stinger when it evolves into Kakuna, but Kakuna doesn't move around much. It is busy evolving into Beedrill. Beedrill is very fast and more poisonous than its pre-evolved forms.

Docile Pidgey would rather not fight. Pidgeotto is much braver. It has great eyesight, and when it evolves into Pidgeot, the super sharp eyesight is combined with extreme speed. Pidgeot can zoom at speeds of Mach 2!

PIDGEY

Tiny Bird Pokémon

Type: Normal/Flying
How to say it: PID-jee
Height: 1' 0"
Weight: 4 lbs
Possible Moves: Tackle, Gust, Quick Attack, Sand-Attack, Whirlwind, Wing Attack, Featherdance, Agility, Mirror Move
Evolves: into Pidgeotto

PIDGEOTTO

Bird Pokémon

Type: Normal/Flying
How to say it: pid-JYO-toe
Height: 3' 7"
Weight: 66 lbs
Possible Moves: Tackle, Gust, Quick Attack, Sand-Attack, Whirlwind, Wing Attack, Featherdance, Agility, Mirror Move
Evolves: into Pidgeot

PIDGEOT

Bird Pokémon

Type: Normal/Flying
How to say it: pid-JEE-ot
Height: 4' 11"
Weight: 87 lbs
Possible Moves: Tackle, Gust, Quick Attack, Sand Attack, Whirlwind, Wing Attack, Featherdance, Agility, Mirror Move
Does not evolve

RATTATA

Mouse Pokémon

Type: Normal
How to say it: ruh-TA-tah
Height: 1' 0"
Weight: 8 lbs
Possible Moves: Tackle, Tail Whip, Quick Attack, Hyper Fang, Focus Energy, Pursuit, Super Fang, Endeavor
Evolves: into Raticate

RATICATE

Mouse Pokémon

Type: Normal
How to say it: RAT-i-kate
Height: 2' 4"
Weight: 41 lbs
Possible Moves: Tackle, Tail Whip, Quick Attack, Hyper Fang, Scary Face, Pursuit, Focus Energy, Super Fang, Endeavor
Does not evolve

SPEAROW

Tiny Bird Pokémon

Type: Normal/Flying
How to say it: SPEER-oh
Height: 1' 0"
Weight: 4 lbs
Possible Moves: Peck, Growl, Pursuit, Aerial Ace, Leer, Fury Attack, Mirror Move, Drill Peck, Agility
Evolves: into Fearow

FEAROW

Beak Pokémon

Type: Normal/Flying
How to say it: FEER-oh
Height: 3' 11"
Weight: 84 lbs
Possible Moves: Peck, Growl, Leer, Fury Attack, Pursuit, Mirror Move, Drill Peck, Agility
Does not evolve

Rattata is a small Pokémon with a big bite. Its fangs are sharp, and Rattata will gnaw on anything. Raticate's fangs never stop growing!

Spearow's loud, shrill cry can be heard for up to half a mile away. And Fearow's long, thin beak is very sharp, so watch out for its Drill Peck attack!

Most Poké-mon are happy to eat berries or Poké Blocks, but Ekans can detach its jaw to swallow prey whole! That's pretty nasty, but Arbok is even more terrifying. The strange pat-terns on its belly hypnotize its prey with fear. Then it wraps its body around its vic-tims—and ends the attack with a poisonous bite.

EKANS

Snake Pokémon

Type: Poison
How to say it: ECK-ehns
Height: 6' 7"
Weight: 15 lbs
Possible Moves: Wrap, Leer, Poison Sting, Bite, Glare, Screech, Acid, Stockpile, Swallow, Spit Up, Haze
Evolves: into Arbok

ARBOK

Snake Pokémon

Type: Poison
How to say it: AR-bock
Height: 11' 6"
Weight: 143 lbs
Possible Moves: Wrap, Leer, Poison Sting, Bite, Glare, Screech, Acid, Swallow, Spit Up, Haze, Stockpile
Does not evolve

Team Rocket's Jessie used to have an Arbok. Then she let Arbok go to be with its own kind. Maybe Jessie isn't as bad as she seems!

PICHU

Tiny Mouse Pokémon

Type: Electric
How to say it: PEE-chew
Height: 1' 0"
Weight: 4 lbs
Possible moves: Thundershock, Charm, Tail Whip, Thunder Wave, Sweet Kiss
Evolves: into Pikachu with Friendship

PIKACHU

Mouse Pokémon

Type: Electric
How to say it: PEEK-uh-chew
Height: 1' 4"
Weight: 13 lbs
Possible Moves: Thundershock, Growl, Tail Whip, Thunder Wave, Quick Attack, Double Team, Agility, Slam, Thunderbolt, Thunder, Light Screen
Evolves: into Raichu with a Thunder Stone

RAICHU

Mouse Pokémon

Type: Electric
How to say it: RYE-chew
Height: 2' 7"
Weight: 66 lbs
Possible moves: Thundershock, Tail Whip, Quick Attack, Thunderbolt
Does not evolve

Tiny Pichu has enough electric power to zap a human adult. Pikachu and Raichu are a lot more powerful. You can catch Pikachu and Raichu in the wild, but there's only one way to get a Pichu: by breeding two Pikachu at a Pokémon Day Care. If you are successful, you will get a Pichu egg, and soon a cute little Pichu will hatch!

Sandshrew can roll itself into a ball to withstand any attack. When Sandshrew evolves into Sandslash, hard spikes cover its body.

SANDSHREW *Mouse Pokémon*

Type: Ground
How to say it: SAND-shroo
Height: 2' 0"
Weight: 26 lbs
Possible Moves: Scratch, Defense Curl, Slash, Poison Sting, Swift, Fury Swipes, Sand Tomb, Sand-Attack, Sandstorm
Evolves: into Sandslash

SANDSLASH *Mouse Pokémon*

Type: Ground
How to say it: SAND-slash
Height: 3' 3"
Weight: 65 lbs
Possible Moves: Scratch, Defense Curl, Sand-Attack, Slash, Poison Sting, Swift, Fury Swipes, Sandstorm, Sand Tomb
Does not evolve

NIDORAN♀ *Poison Pin Pokémon*

Type: Poison
How to say it: nee-door-ANN
Height: 1' 4"
Weight: 15 lbs
Possible Moves: Growl, Scratch, Poison Sting, Tail Whip, Bite, Helping Hand, Fury Swipes, Double Kick, Flatter, Crunch
Evolves: into Nidorina

NIDORINA *Poison Pin Pokémon*

Type: Poison
How to say it: nee-door-EE-nuh
Height: 2' 7"
Weight: 44 lbs
Possible Moves: Growl, Scratch, Poison Sting, Tail Whip, Bite, Helping Hand, Fury Swipes, Double Kick, Flatter, Crunch
Evolves: into Nidoqueen with a Moon Stone

NIDOQUEEN *Drill Pokémon*

Type: Poison/Ground
How to say it: nee-doe-QUEEN
Height: 4' 3"
Weight: 132 lbs
Possible Moves: Scratch, Tail Whip, Double Kick, Poison Sting, Body Slam, Superpower
Does not evolve

Nidoran does not like to fight, but be careful—just a scratch from her poisonous spikes can make you sick! Nidorina keeps her spikes tucked away when she is around family, so she won't hurt them. Nidoqueen protects her family, too. She is strongest when keeping her young safe from enemies.

The bodies of these Pokémon are built for battle. Nidoran and Nidorino use their big ears to sense if enemies are nearby. Nidoking uses its thick tail to smash its opponents. And all three use their hard, sharp horn to deliver devastating attacks.

NIDORAN ♂

Poison Pin Pokémon

Type: Poison
How to say it: nee-door-ANN
Height: 1' 8"
Weight: 20 lbs
Possible Moves: Leer, Peck, Horn Attack, Helping Hand, Poison Sting, Focus Energy, Flatter, Fury Attack, Horn Drill, Double Kick
Evolves: into Nidorino

NIDORINO

Poison Pin Pokémon

Type: Poison
How to say it: nee-door-EE-no
Height: 2' 11"
Weight: 43 lbs
Possible Moves: Leer, Peck, Horn Attack, Poison Sting, Focus Energy, Fury Attack, Horn Drill, Double Kick, Helping Hand, Flatter
Evolves: into Nidoking

NIDOKING

Drill Pokémon

Type: Poison/Ground
How to say it: nee-doe-KING
Height: 4' 7"
Weight: 137 lbs
Possible Moves: Peck, Focus Energy, Poison Sting, Thrash, Double Kick, Megahorn
Does not evolve

CLEFFA

Fairy Pokémon

Type: Normal
How to say it: clef-FA
Height: 1' 0"
Weight: 7 lbs
Possible Moves: Pound, Charm, Encore, Sing, Sweet Kiss, Magical Leaf
Evolves: into

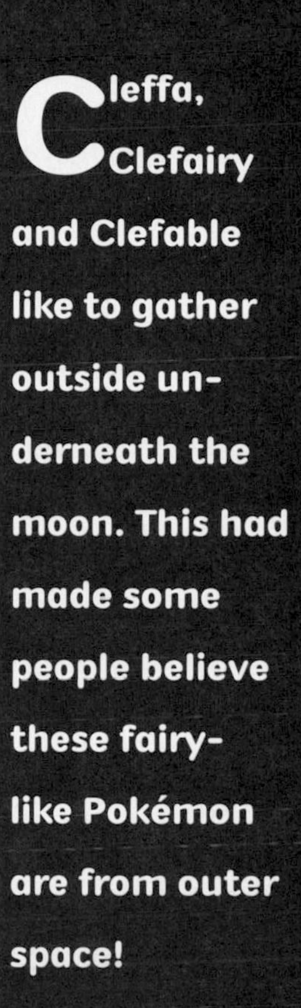

Cleffa, Clefairy and Clefable like to gather outside underneath the moon. This had made some people believe these fairy-like Pokémon are from outer space!

CLEFAIRY

Fairy Pokémon

Type: Normal
How to say it: cluh-FAIR-ee
Height: 2' 0"
Weight: 17 lbs
Possible Moves: Pound, Growl, Encore, Sing, Doubleslap, Follow Me, Minimize, Metronome, Defense Curl, Cosmic Power, Light Screen, Moonlight
Evolves: into Clefable with a Moon Stone

CLEFABLE

Fairy Pokémon

Type: Normal
How to say it: cluh-FAY-bull
Height: 4' 3"
Weight: 88 lbs
Possible Moves: Sing, Doubleslap, Minimize, Metronome
Does not evolve

Vulpix has six beautiful tails. Its evolved form, Ninetales, has nine tails that are supposed to hold supernatural powers. They are said to be able to keep Ninetales alive for 1,000 years.

VULPIX

Fox Pokémon

Type: Fire
How to say it: VULL-picks
Height: 2' 0"
Weight: 22 lbs
Attacks: Ember, Tail Whip, Quick Attack, Will-O-Wisp, Confuse Ray, Safeguard, Roar, Flamethrower, Grudge, Fire Spin
Evolves: into Ninetales with a Fire Stone

NINETALES

Fox Pokémon

Type: Fire
How to say it: NINE-tails
Height: 3' 7"
Weight: 44 lbs
Possible Moves: Fire Spin, Ember, Quick Attack, Confuse Ray, Safeguard
Does not evolve

IGGLYBUFF *Balloon Pokémon*

Type: Normal
How to say it: igg-lee-BUFF
Height: 1' 0"
Weight: 2 lbs
Possible Moves: Sing, Charm, Defense Curl, Pound, Sweet Kiss
Evolves: into Jigglypuff with Friendship

JIGGLYPUFF *Balloon Pokémon*

Type: Normal
How to say it: jig-lee-PUFF
Height: 1' 8"
Weight: 12 lbs
Possible Moves: Sing, Pound, Disable, Defense Curl, Rollout, Doubleslap, Rest, Body Slam, Mimic, Hyper Voice, Double Edge
Evolves: into Wigglytuff with a Moon Stone

WIGGLYTUFF *Balloon Pokémon*

Type: Normal
How to say it: wig-lee-TUFF
Height: 3' 3"
Weight: 26 lbs
Possible Moves: Sing, Disable, Defense Curl, Doubleslap
Does not evolve

Jigglypuff is famous for its beautiful song. But it's more like a lullaby, because Jigglypuff's song puts everyone to sleep. You need a Moon Stone to evolve Jifflypuff into Wigglytuff. And if you've got both a Jigglypuff and a Wigglytuff, you might be able to breed them to get a bouncy little Igglybuff!

The best time to find these Pokémon is at night. Zubat can fly in dark places because it emits ultrasonic waves to check for objects in its way. Golbat flies around at night, looking for fresh blood—its favorite snack. When it evolves into Crobat, it develops extra wings on its legs so it can fly faster.

ZUBAT

Bat Pokémon

Type: Poison/Flying
How to say it: ZOO-bat
Height: 2' 7"
Weight: 17 lbs
Possible Moves: Leech Life, Astonish, Supersonic, Bite, Confuse Ray, Wing Attack, Air Cutter, Haze, Mean Look, Poison Fang
Evolves: into Golbat

GOLBAT

Bat Pokémon

Type: Poison/Flying
How to say it: GOAL-bat
Height: 5' 3"
Weight: 121 lbs
Possible Moves: Leech Life, Screech, Astonish, Supersonic, Bite, Confuse Ray, Wing Attack, Air Cutter, Mean Look, Poison Fang, Haze
Evolves: into Crobat with Friendship

CROBAT

Bat Pokémon

Type: Poison/Flying
How to say it: CROW-bat
Height: 5' 11"
Weight: 165 lbs
Possible Moves: Screech, Leech Life, Astonish, Bite, Wing Attack, Supersonic, Confuse Ray, Air Cutter, Mean Look, Poison Fang, Haze
Does not evolve

ODDISH

Weed Pokémon

Type: Grass/Poison
How to say it: ODD-ish
Height: 1' 8"
Weight: 12 lbs
Possible Moves: Absorb, Sweet Scent, Poisonpowder, Stun Spore, Sleep Powder, Acid, Moonlight, Petal Dance
Evolves: into Gloom

GLOOM

Weed Pokémon

Type: Grass/Poison
How to say it: GLOOM
Height: 2' 7"
Weight: 19 lbs
Possible Moves: Absorb, Sweet Scent, Poisonpowder, Stun Spore, Sleep Powder, Acid, Moonlight, Petal Dance
Evolves: into Vileplume using a Leaf Stone, or into Bellossom using a Sun Stone

VILEPLUME

Flower Pokémon

Type: Grass/Poison
How to say it: VILE-ploom
Height: 3' 11"
Weight: 41 lbs
Possible Moves: Absorb, Aromatherapy, Mega Drain, Petal Dance, Stun Spore
Does not evolve

BELLOSSOM

Flower Pokémon

Type: Grass
How to say it: bell-OSS-uhm
Height: 1' 4"
Weight: 13 lbs
Possible Moves: Absorb, Sweet Scent, Stun Spore, Magical Leaf, Petal Dance, Solarbeam
Does not evolve

After cute Oddish evolves into stinky Gloom, you get to decide what happens next. You can use a Leaf Stone to evolve it into terribly toxic Vileplume. Or use a Sun Stone to get adorable Bellossom. Poisonous or pretty? It's up to you!

The mushrooms on Paras's back are parasites that feed off the Bug Pokémon. Eventually, the mushrooms take over its entire body. This is when Paras evolves into Parasect.

PARAS

Mushroom Pokémon

Type: Bug/Grass
How to say it: PAR-iss
Height: 1' 0"
Weight: 12 lbs
Possible Moves: Scratch, Stun Spore, Poisonpowder, Leech Life, Spore, Slash, Growth, Giga Drain, Aromatherapy
Evolves: into Parasect

PARASECT

Mushroom Pokémon

Type: Bug/Grass
How to say it: PAR-i-sect
Height: 3' 3"
Weight: 65 lbs
Possible Moves: Scratch, Stun Spore, Poisonpowder, Leech Life, Spore, Slash, Growth, Giga Drain, Aromatherapy
Does not evolve

VENONAT *Insect Pokémon*

Type: Bug/Poison
How to say it: VENN-oh-nat
Height: 3' 3"
Weight: 33 lbs
Possible Moves: Tackle, Disable, Foresight, Supersonic, Confusion, Poisonpowder, Leech Life, Stun Spore, Psybeam, Sleep Powder, Psychic
Evolves: into Venomoth

VENOMOTH *Poison Moth Pokémon*

Type: Bug/Poison
How to say it: VENN-oh-moth
Height: 4' 11"
Weight: 28 lbs
Possible Moves: Silver Wind, Tackle, Disable, Foresight, Supersonic, Confusion, Poisonpowder, Leech Life, Stun Spore, Gust, Psybeam, Sleep Powder, Psychic
Does not evolve

The buglike Venonat sleeps during the day but comes out when it's dark to eat nighttime insects. Venomoth's wings are covered in powdery scales that contain poison.

A farmer's best friend, Diglett lives underground digging holes and making the soil perfect for planting. Dugtrio isn't as popular. The three-headed Pokémon burrows at over 60 mph and triggers small earthquakes.

DIGLETT

Mole Pokémon

Type: Ground
How to say it: DIG-lit
Height: 0' 8"
Weight: 2 lbs
Possible Moves: Scratch, Growl, Dig, Sand-Attack, Magnitude, Fury Swipes, Slash, Earthquake, Mud-Slap, Fissure
Evolves: into Dugtrio

DUGTRIO

Mole Pokémon

Type: Ground
How to say it: dug-TREE-oh
Height: 2' 4"
Weight: 73 lbs
Possible Moves: Tri Attack, Scratch, Growl, Magnitude, Dig, Sand-Attack, Fury Swipes, Slash, Earthquake, Mud-Slap, Sand Tomb, Fissure
Does not evolve

MEOWTH

Scratch Cat Pokémon

Type: Normal
How to say it: me-OUTH
Height: 1' 4"
Weight: 9 lbs
Possible Moves: Scratch, Growl, Bite, Pay Day, Faint Attack, Screech, Fury Swipes, Slash, Fake Out, Swagger
Evolves: into Persian

PERSIAN

Classy Cat Pokémon

Type: Normal
How to say it: PURR-shin
Height: 3' 3"
Weight: 71 lbs
Possible Moves: Scratch, Growl, Bite, Pay Day, Faint Attack, Screech, Fury Swipes, Slash, Fake Out, Swagger
Does not evolve

The most famous Meowth of all belongs to Team Rocket. This talking troublemaker dreams of stealing rare Pokémon.

Most Meowth can't talk like Team Rocket's can. It's no wonder a Meowth joined up with the group of thieves. These Pokémon love bright shiny coins! Persian is a sleek, elegant cat. But its elegance hides a wild side. Persian will gladly rip apart its enemies.

Psyduck almost always has a headache. When its headache gets really bad, wham! Psyduck lets loose some amazing powers. But most of the time, the headaches just make Psyduck confused and clumsy. There is nothing clumsy about Golduck, however. It's a graceful Pokémon with mysterious telekinetic powers.

PSYDUCK *Duck Pokémon*

Type: Water
How to say it: SYE-duck
Height: 2' 7"
Weight: 43 lbs
Possible Moves: Water Sport, Scratch, Tail Whip, Disable, Confusion, Screech, Psych Up, Fury Swipes, Hydro Pump
Evolves: into Golduck

GOLDUCK *Duck Pokémon*

Type: Water
How to say it: GOAL-duck
Height: 5' 7"
Weight: 169 lbs
Possible Moves: Water Sport, Scratch, Tail Whip, Disable, Confusion, Screech, Psych Up, Fury Swipes, Hydro Pump
Does not evolve

Psyduck may get terrible headaches, but it's nothing like the pain it gives Misty! Psyduck always pops out of its Poké Ball at the worst times!

MANKEY

Pig Monkey Pokémon

Type: Fighting
How to say it: MANK-ee
Height: 1' 8"
Weight: 62 lbs
Possible Moves: Scratch, Leer, Low Kick, Karate Chop, Fury Swipes, Swagger, Screech, Focus Energy, Seismic Toss, Cross Chop, Thrash
Evolves: into Primeape

PRIMEAPE

Pig Monkey Pokémon

Type: Fighting
How to say it: PRIME-ape
Height: 3' 3"
Weight: 71 lbs
Possible Moves: Scratch, Leer, Low Kick, Rage, Karate Chop, Fury Swipes, Focus Energy, Seismic Toss, Swagger, Screech, Cross Chop, Thrash
Does not evolve

The Fighting Pokémon Mankey is famous for its terrible temper. But when it evolves into Primeape, it becomes even angrier. If you even look at Primeape the wrong way, it won't stop chasing you until it's got you cornered.

Growlithe are very friendly, and very loyal to their trainers. They will bark fiercely to protect their Trainers from danger. Its evolved form, Arcanine, has long been admired for its beauty and speed. It is said that fire runs through its body, giving it power.

GROWLITHE

Puppy Pokémon

Type: Fire
How to say it: GROWL-ith
Height: 2' 4"
Weight: 42 lbs
Possible Moves: Bite, Roar, Ember, Leer, Odor Sleuth, Take Down, Flame Wheel, Helping Hand, Agility, Flamethrower
Evolves: into Arcanine using a Fire Stone

ARCANINE

Legendary Pokémon

Type: Fire
How to say it: ar-kuh-NINE
Height: 6' 3"
Weight: 342 lbs
Possible moves: Bite, Roar, Ember, Odor Sleuth, Extremespeed
Does not evolve

POLIWAG *Tadpole Pokémon*

Type: Water
How to say it: POL-ee-wag
Height: 2' 0"
Weight: 27 lbs
Possible Moves: Bubble, Hypnosis, Water Gun, Doubleslap, Rain Dance, Belly Drum, Body Slam, Hydro Pump
Evolves: into Poliwhirl

POLIWHIRL *Tadpole Pokémon*

Type: Water
How to say it: POL-ee-wurl
Height: 3' 3"
Weight: 44 lbs
Possible Moves: Bubble, Hypnosis, Water Gun, Doubleslap, Rain Dance, Belly Drum, Body Slam, Amnesia, Hydro Pump
Evolves: into Politoed if traded while holding a King's Rock and a Trade, and into Poliwrath with a Water Stone

POLIWRATH *Tadpole Pokémon*

Type: Water/Fighting
How to say it: POL-ee-rath
Height: 4' 3"
Weight: 119 lbs
Possible Moves: Hypnosis, Water Gun, Doubleslap, Submission, Mind Reader
Does not evolve

POLITOED *Frog Pokémon*

Type: Water
How to say it: POLY-toad
Height: 3' 7"
Weight: 75 lbs
Possible Moves: Water Gun, Hypnosis, Doubleslap, Perish Song, Swagger
Does not evolve

If you like Water Pokémon, take the plunge and catch a Poliwag! This little guy evolves into Poliwhirl, which puts its opponents to sleep with the spiral markings on its belly. Then you can use a Water Stone to get a tough Poliwrath, or a King's Rock to get a cute Politoed. Either way, you can't lose!

Abra sleeps for 18 hours a day. If it senses danger when it's sleeping, it will teleport itself away to safety. Kadabra, the evolved form of Abra, emits a powerful alpha wave from its body. This wave can give anyone nearby a headache. Alakazam is a super smart Pokémon. It has an IQ of 5,000!

ABRA

Psi Pokémon

Type: Psychic
How to say it: AB-ruh
Height: 2' 11"
Weight: 43 lbs
Possible Moves: Teleport
Evolves: into Kadabra

KADABRA

Psi Pokémon

Type: Psychic
How to say it: kah-DA-bruh
Height: 4' 3"
Weight: 125 lbs
Possible Moves: Teleport, Confusion, Disable, Psybeam, Recover, Psychic, Reflect
Evolves: into Alakazam

ALAKAZAM

Psi Pokémon

Type: Psychic
How to say it: al-uh-kuh-ZAM
Height: 4' 11"
Weight: 106 lbs
Possible Moves: Teleport, Kinesis, Confusion, Disable, Psybeam, Recover, Future Sight, Calm Mind, Trick, Psychic, Reflect
Does not evolve

MACHOP

Superpower Pokémon

Type: Fighting
How to say it: MAH-chop
Height: 2' 7"
Weight: 43 lbs
Possible Moves: Karate Chop, Low Kick, Leer, Focus Energy, Seismic Toss, Foresight, Revenge, Vital Throw, Submission, Cross Chop, Scary Face, Dynamicpunch
Evolves: into Machoke

MACHOKE

Superpower Pokémon

Type: Fighting
How to say it: MAH-choke
Height: 4' 1"
Weight: 155 lbs
Possible Moves: Karate Chop, Low Kick, Leer, Focus Energy, Seismic Toss, Foresight, Revenge, Submission, Vital Throw, Cross Chop, Scary Face, Dynamicpunch
Evolves: into Machamp

MACHAMP

Superpower Pokémon

Type: Fighting
How to say it: MAH-champ
Height: 5' 3"
Weight: 287 lbs
Possible Moves: Karate Chop, Low Kick, Leer, Focus Energy, Seismic Toss, Foresight, Revenge, Vital Throw, Submission, Cross Chop, Scary Face, Dynamicpunch
Does not evolve

Machop may be small, but this fighting Pokémon loves to work out any chance it can get. Machop gets even more muscular when it evolves into Machoke. Machoke has muscles of steel and when it evolves into Machamp, it gets two more powerful, muscular arms. Machamp can throw punches at lightning speed.

If you find these carnivorous Grass/Poison Pokémon in your garden, look out! Bell-sprout likes to trap bugs and eat them. Weepinbell sprays its enemies with Acid. And Victreebel's mouth is big enough to swallow its prey whole. Just ask James from Team Rocket!

BELLSPROUT *Flower Pokémon*

Type: Grass/Poison
How to say it: BELL-sprout
Height: 2' 4"
Weight: 9 lbs
Possible Moves: Vine Whip, Growth, Wrap, Poisonpowder, Sleep Powder, Stun Spore, Acid, Razor Leaf, Slam, Sweet Scent
Evolves: into Weepinbell

WEEPINBELL *Flycatcher Pokémon*

Type: Grass/Poison
How to say it: WEEP-in-bell
Height: 3' 3"
Weight: 14 lbs
Possible Moves: Vine Whip, Growth, Wrap, Poisonpowder, Sleep Powder, Stun Spore, Acid, Razor Leaf, Slam, Sweet Scent
Evolves: into Victreebel with a Leaf Stone

VICTREEBEL *Flycatcher Pokémon*

Type: Grass/Poison
How to say it: VICK-tree-bell
Height: 5' 7"
Weight: 34 lbs
Possible Moves: Poisonpowder, Sleep Powder, Stockpile, Spit Up, Swallow, Vine Whip, Sweet Scent, Razor Leaf
Does not evolve

TENTACOOL *Jellyfish Pokémon*

Type: Water/Poison
How to say it: TENT-uh-cool
Height: 2' 11"
Weight: 100 lbs
Possible Moves: Acid, Supersonic, Bubblebeam, Wrap, Poison Sting, Constrict, Barrier, Screech, Hydro Pump
Evolves: into Tentacruel

TENTACRUEL *Jellyfish Pokémon*

Type: Water/Poison
How to say it: TENT-uh-crool
Height: 5' 3"
Weight: 121 lbs
Possible Moves: Acid, Supersonic, Wrap, Bubblebeam, Poison Sting, Constrict, Barrier, Screech, Hydro Pump
Does not evolve

Battling a Charmeleon? Throw out a Tentacruel or another Water Type Pokémon. Water Types have an advantage over Fire Types.

Tentacool need water to survive. If you find a dried-up Tentacool on the beach, toss it back in the sea and watch it revive! But you might not want to get too near Tentacruel. It likes to wrap its prey in a dangerous net of 80 poison tentacles!

Geodude may look like a big rock, but don't step on it! You'll just make it angry. And a Graveler will just run you over if you're in its way—they can roll down mountain paths at fast speeds. And you definitely don't want to be in Golem's path—at a whopping 622 lbs, it is like a huge boulder!

GEODUDE

Rock Pokémon

Type: Rock/Ground
How to say it: JEE-oh-dood
Height: 1' 4"
Weight: 44 lbs
Possible Moves: Tackle, Defense Curl, Mud Sport, Rock Throw, Selfdestruct, Magnitude, Rollout, Rock Blast, Earthquake, Explosion, Double-Edge
Evolves: into Graveler

GRAVELER

Rock Pokémon

Type: Rock/Ground
How to say it: GRAV-el-er
Height: 3' 3"
Weight: 232 lbs
Possible Moves: Tackle, Defense Curl, Mud Sport, Magnitude, Rock Throw, Selfdestruct, Rollout, Earthquake, Rock Blast, Explosion, Double-Edge
Evolves: into Golem

GOLEM

Megaton Pokémon

Type: Rock/Ground
How to say it: GOAL-um
Height: 4' 7"
Weight: 622 lbs
Possible Moves: Tackle, Defense Curl, Mud Sport, Rock Throw, Magnitude, Selfdestruct, Rollout, Rock Blast, Earthquake, Explosion, Double-Edge
Does not evolve

PONYTA

Fire Horse Pokémon

Type: Fire
How to say it: po-NEE-tuh
Height: 3' 3"
Weight: 66 lbs
Possible moves: Quick Attack, Ember, Tail Whip, Stomp, Growl, Fire Spin, Take Down, Fire Blast, Agility, Bounce
Evolves: into Rapidash

RAPIDASH

Fire Horse Pokémon

Type: Fire
How to say it: RAP-i-dash
Height: 5' 7"
Weight: 209 lbs
Possible moves: Quick Attack, Ember, Tail Whip, Stomp, Growl, Fire Spin, Take Down, Agility, Fury Attack, Bounce, Fire Blast
Does not evolve

When a Ponyta is born, it can barely stand. But soon it is jumping high and running fast. And Rapidash loves to run so much, it will race anything it can! Its fiery mane blazes as it reaches speeds up to 150 mph.

Slowpoke does everything slowly. After it's attacked, it takes an average of five seconds before it even knows it's in pain. For Slowpoke to evolve into Slowbro, it has to stick its tail in the water. If a Shellder bites it, you're in luck! Slowpoke will become Slowbro.

SLOWPOKE *Dopey Pokémon*

Type: Water/Psychic
How to say it: SLOW-poke
Height: 3' 11"
Weight: 79 lbs
Possible moves: Cure, Yawn, Tackle, Confusion, Disable, Headbutt, Growl, Water Gun, Amnesia, Psychic, Psych Up
Evolves: into Slowpoke

SLOWBRO *Hermit Crab Pokémon*

Type: Water/Psychic
How to say it: SLOW-bro
Height: 5' 3"
Weight: 173 lbs
Possible moves: Curse, Yawn, Tackle, Confusion, Disable, Headbutt, Growl, Water Gun, Withdraw, Amnesia, Psychic, Psych Up
Evolves: into Slowking

SLOWKING *Royal Pokémon*

Type: Water-Psychic
How to say it: SLOW-king
Height: 6' 7"
Weight: 175 lbs
Possible Moves: Oblivious, Own Tempo
Does not evolve

MAGNEMITE *Magnet Pokémon*

Type: Electric/Steel
How to say it: MAG-nuh-mite
Height: 1' 0"
Weight: 13 lbs
Possible moves: Metal Sound, Tackle, Sonicboom, Thundershock, Supersonic, Thunder Wave, Spark, Lock-On, Swift, Screech, Zap Cannon
Evolves: into Magneton

MAGNETON *Magnet Pokémon*

Type: Electric/Steel
How to say it: MAG-nuh-tun
Height: 3' 3"
Weight: 132 lbs
Possible moves: Metal Sound, Tackle, Sonicboom, Thundershock, Supersonic, Thunder Wave, Spark, Lock-On, Tri Attack, Zap Cannon, Screech
Does not evolve

If you have an Electric Pokémon, why not teach it Flash? You can use this move to light up dark caves.

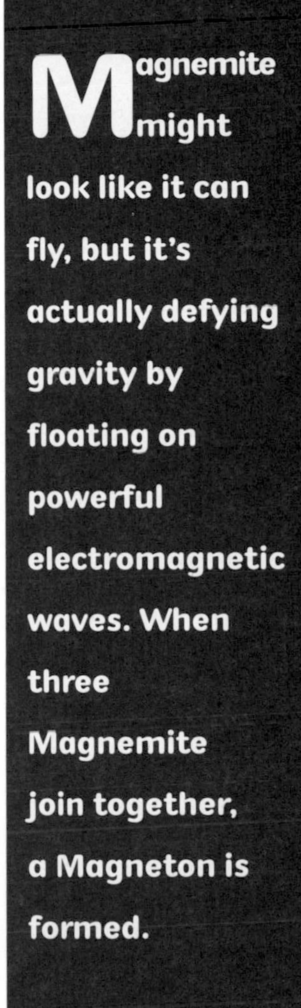

Magnemite might look like it can fly, but it's actually defying gravity by floating on powerful electromagnetic waves. When three Magnemite join together, a Magneton is formed.

The ducklike Pokémon Farfetch'd is always seen carrying a stick—usually a sprig of green onion—in its mouth. It will fight with other Farfetch'd over the best sticks.

Doduo's two heads never sleep at the same time. One head stays awake to watch out for enemies. Doduo gets an extra head when it evolves into Dodrio. Dodrio is very smart and, like Doduo, it keeps one head on guard while the others sleep.

FARFETCH'D *Wild Duck*

Type: Normal/Flying
How to say it: FAR-fetcht
Height: 2' 7"
Weight: 33 lbs
Possible Moves: Peck, Sand-Attack, Leer, Fury Attack, Knock Off, Fury Cutter, Swords Dance, Agility, Slash, False Swipe
Does not evolve

DODUO *Twin Bird Pokémon*

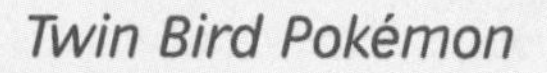

Type: Normal/Flying
How to say it: DOE-doo-oh
Height: 4' 7"
Weight: 86 lbs
Possible Moves: Peck, Fury Attack, Pursuit, Drill Peck, Rage, Tri Attack, Growl, Agility, Uproar
Evolves: into Dodrio

DODRIO *Triple Bird Pokémon*

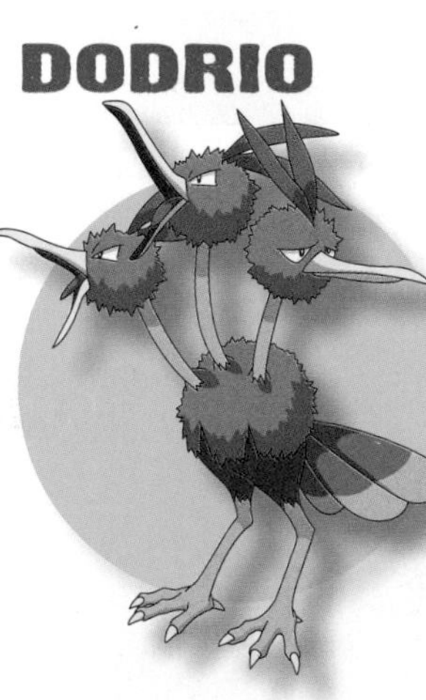

Type: Normal/Flying
How to say it: doe-DREE-oh
Height: 5' 11"
Weight: 188 lbs
Possible Moves: Peck, Growl, Pursuit, Fury Attack, Drill Peck, Rage, Tri Attack, Uproar, Agility
Does not evolve

SEEL *Sea Lion Pokémon*

Type: Water
How to say it: SEEL
Height: 3' 7"
Weight: 198 lbs
Possible Moves: Headbutt, Aurora Beam, Rest, Take Down, Ice Beam, Safeguard, Growl, Icy Wind
Evolves: into Dewgong

DEWGONG *Sea Lion Pokémon*

Type: Water/Ice
How to say it: DOO-gong
Height: 5' 7"
Weight: 265 lbs
Possible Moves: Single Beam, Headbutt, Growl, Icy Wind, Aurora Beam, Sheer Cold, Rest, Take Down, Ice Beam, Safeguard
Does not evolve

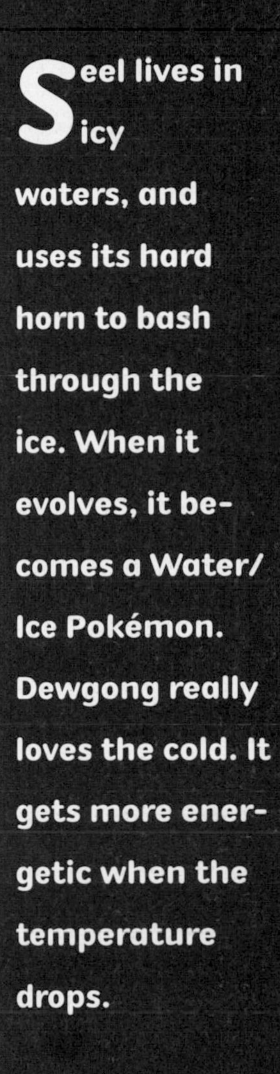

Seel lives in icy waters, and uses its hard horn to bash through the ice. When it evolves, it becomes a Water/Ice Pokémon. Dewgong really loves the cold. It gets more energetic when the temperature drops.

Is the Pokémon you want to catch under water? Try a Dive Ball!

Grimer smells terrible! Maybe it's because it lives in filthy sludge. Muk is even worse. Just smelling it can make you faint! And if you touch it by accident, its powerful poison will give you a fever.

GRIMER

Sludge Pokémon

Type: Poison
How to say it: GRIME-er
Height: 2' 11"
Weight: 66 lbs
Possible Moves: Pound, Disable, Poison Gas, Minimize, Sludge, Harden, Screech, Acid Armor, Sludge Bomb, Memento
Evolves: into Muk

MUK

Sludge Pokémon

Type: Poison
How to say it: MUCK
Height: 3' 11"
Weight: 66 lbs
Possible Moves: Pound, Disable, Poison Gas, Sludge Bomb, Minimize, Sludge, Harden, Screech, Acid Armor, Memento
Does not evolve

SHELLDER *Bivalve Pokémon*

Type: Water
How to say it: SHELL-der
Height: 1' 0"
Weight: 9 lbs
Possible Moves: Tackle, Withdraw, Icicle Spear, Supersonic, Clamp, Aurora Beam, Protect, Leer, Ice Beam
Evolves: into Cloyster with a Water Stone

CLOYSTER *Bivalve Pokémon*

Type: Water/Ice
How to say it: CLOY-stir
Height: 4' 11"
Weight: 292 lbs
Possible Moves: Withdraw, Supersonic, Aurora Beam, Protect, Spikes, Spike Cannon
Does not evolve

Shellder's hard shell can withstand any attack. The best time to attack it is when its shell is open. Cloyster's shell is even more amazing. This Water Pokémon can shoot sharp spikes from its shell, so watch out!

This is one terrifying trio of Poké-mon! With its light body, Gastly can sneak into any place it wants. Haunter waits in the dark, hoping to lick victims with its gaseous tongue. And Gengar hides in the shad-ows, ready to jump out and frighten its victims. That's pretty scary!

GASTLY

Gas Pokémon

Type: Ghost/Poison
How to say it: GAST-lee
Height: 4' 3"
Weight: 0.2 lbs
Possible Moves: Lick, Spite, Curse, Confuse Ray, Night Shade, Hypnosis, Dream Eater, Destiny Bond, Shadow Ball, Nightmare, Mean Look
Evolves: into Haunter

HAUNTER

Gas Pokémon

Type: Ghost/Poison
How to say it: HAWN-ter
Height: 5' 3"
Weight: 0.2 lbs
Possible Moves: Lick, Confuse Ray, Night Shade, Hypnosis, Dream Eater, Spite, Curse, Shad-ow Punch, Destiny Bond, Shadow Ball, Nightmare, Mean Look
Evolves: into Gengar

GENGAR

Shadow Pokémon

Type: Ghost/Poison
How to say it: GANG-are
Height: 4' 11"
Weight: 89 lbs
Possible Moves: Lick, Con-fuse Ray, Night Shade, Hypno-sis, Dream Eater, Spite, Curse, Shadow Punch, Destiny Bond, Shadow Ball, Nightmare, Mean Look
Does not evolve

ONIX

Rock Snake Pokémon

Type: Rock/Ground
How to say it: ON-icks
Height: 28' 10"
Weight: 463 lbs
Possible Moves: Tackle, Screech, Bind, Rock Throw, Rage, Slam, Harden, Dragonbreath, Sandstorm, Iron Tail, Sand Tomb, Double-Edge
Evolves: into Steelix

STEELIX

Iron Snake Pokémon

Type: Steel-Ground
How to say it: STEAL-icks
Height: 30' 2"
Weight: 882 lbs
Possible Moves: Tackle, Screech, Bind, Rock Throw, Harden, Rage, Dragonbreath, Sandstorm, Slam, Iron Tail, Crunch, Double-Edge
Does not evolve

Onix's body is so hard that the stone becomes like black diamonds over time. It can dig through the ground as fast as 50 mph!

Drowzee loves to eat dreams. If you had a great dream you just can't remember, chances are a Drowzee sucked it through your nostrils while you were sleeping. If Hypno is hungry, it will put you to sleep with its pendulum. Then it will munch on your dreams!

DROWZEE

Hypnosis Pokémon

Type: Psychic
How to say it: DROW-zee
Height: 3' 3"
Weight: 71 lbs
Possible Moves: Pound, Hypnosis, Disable, Confusion, Headbutt, Poison Gas, Psychic, Meditate, Psych Up, Swagger, Future Sight
Evolves: into Hypno

HYPNO

Hypnosis Pokémon

Type: Psychic
How to say it: HIP-no
Height: 5' 3"
Weight: 167 lbs
Possible Moves: Nightmare, Pound, Hypnosis, Disable, Confusion, Headbutt, Poison Gas, Psychic, Meditate, Psych Up, Swagger, Future Sight
Does not evolve

KRABBY

River Crab Pokémon

Type: Water
How to say it: CRA-bee
Height: 1' 4"
Weight: 14 lbs
Possible Moves: Bubble, Leer, Vicegrip, Mud Shot, Guillotine, Stomp, Crabhammer, Harden, Protect, Flail
Evolves: into Kingler

KINGLER

Pincer Pokémon

Type: Water
How to say it: KING-ler
Height: 4' 3"
Weight: 132 lbs
Possible Moves: Metal Claw, Bubble, Leer, Vicegrip, Guillotine, Protect, Flail, Stomp, Crabhammer, Harden, Mud Shot
Does not evolve

If one of Krabby's pincers falls off during battle, it can quickly grow a new one. When it evolves into Kingler, its claws become as hard as steel. They can crush almost anything, but they are heavy and difficult for Kingler to use.

Voltorb and Electrode may look like Poké Balls, but they are very dangerous to handle. Both of them can explode at almost any time!

VOLTORB *Ball Pokémon*

Type: Electric
How to say it: VOL-torb
Height: 1' 8"
Weight: 23 lbs
Possible moves: Charge, Tackle, Screech, Sonicboom, Spark, Selfdestruct, Rollout, Light Screen, Swift, Explosion, Mirror Coat
Evolves: into Electrode

ELECTRODE *Ball Pokémon*

Type: Electric
How to say it: ee-LECK-trode
Height: 3' 11"
Weight: 147 lbs
Possible moves: Charge, Tackle, Screech, Sonicboom, Spark, Selfdestruct, Rollout, Light Screen, Swift, Explosion, Mirror Coat
Does not evolve

EXEGGCUTE *Egg Pokémon*

Type: Grass/Psychic
How to say it: EGGS-egg-cute
Height: 1' 4"
Weight: 6 lbs
Possible Moves: Barrage, Uproar, Hypnosis, Reflect, Leech Seed, Confusion, Stun Spore, Poisonpowder, Solar Beam, Sleep Powder
Evolves: into Exeggutor with a Leaf Stone

EXEGGUTOR *Coconut Pokémon*

Type: Grass/Psychic
How to say it: EGGS-egg-you-tor
Height: 6' 7"
Weight: 265 lbs
Possible Moves: Barrage, Hypnosis, Confusion, Stomp, Egg Bomb
Does not evolve

You can teach some of your Pokémon a move called Egg Bomb. It allows your Pokémon to hurl exploding eggs at its opponents!

Exeggcute looks a lot like a bunch of eggs. You will always find six Exeggcute grouped together. When Exeggcute evolves, it becomes Exeggutor, a strange-looking Pokémon with three heads. Some people say that if one of Exeggutor's heads falls off, the head will become an Exeggcute!

Because Cubone always wears its skull helmet, no one knows what its face looks like. This sad Pokémon cries all the time. But when it evolves into Marowak, it is tough and ready for battle.

CUBONE

Lonely Pokémon

Type: Ground
How to say it: CUE-bone
Height: 1' 4"
Weight: 14 lbs
Possible Moves: Bone Club, Growl, Tail Whip, Headbutt, Leer, Focus Energy, Thrash, False Swipe, Bonemerang, Rage, Bone Rush, Double-Edge
Evolves: into Marowak

MAROWAK

Bone Keeper Pokémon

Type: Ground
How to say it: MAR-row-ack
Height: 3' 3"
Weight: 99 lbs
Possible Moves: Bone Club, Growl, Tail Whip, Headbutt, Leer, Focus Energy, Thrash, Bonemerang, Rage, False Swipe, Bone Rush, Double-Edge
Does not evolve

TYROGUE *Scuffle Pokémon*

Type: Fighting
How to say it: tie-ROGUE
Height: 2' 4"
Weight: 46 lbs
Possible Moves: Tackle
Evolves: Hitmonlee, Hitmonchan, or Hitmontop

HITMONLEE *Kicking Pokémon*

Type: Fighting
How to say it: HIT-moan-lee
Height: 4' 11"
Weight: 110 lbs
Possible Moves: Revenge, Meditate, Rolling Kick, Brick Break, Double Kick, Jump Kick, Focus Energy, Hi Jump Kick, Mind Reader, Foresight, Endure, Mega Kick, Reversal
Does not evolve

HITMONCHAN *Punching Pokémon*

Type: Fighting
How to say it: HIT-moan-chan
Height: 4' 7"
Weight: 111 lbs
Possible Moves: Revenge, Comet Punch, Agility, Pursuit, Mach Punch, Fire Punch, Ice Punch, Thunderpunch, Sky Uppercut, Mega Punch, Detect, Counter
Does not evolve

HITMONTOP *Handstand Pokémon*

Type: Fighting
How to say it: HIT-mown-top
Height: 4' 7"
Weight: 105 lbs
Possible Moves: Revenge, Rolling Kick, Focus Energy, Pursuit, Quick Attack, Triple Kick, Rapid Spin, Counter, Agility, Detect, Endeavor
Does not evolve

Hitmonlee is famous for its fast and furious kicks. Hitmonchan fires nonstop punches at its opponent. And Hitmontop delivers kicks as it spins on top of its head. You will need to breed a Hitmonlee or a Hitmonchan with a Ditto to get a Tyrogue. Depending on how you train it, Tyrogue will evolve into Hitmonlee, Hitmonchan, or Hitmontop.

Lickitung's sticky tongue is almost 7 feet long! It uses its tongue to learn about new things by licking them.

What's that smell? It might be Koffing, releasing toxic gas. When two kinds of poisonous gas meet, two Koffings will fuse together to become a Weezing.

LICKITUNG *Licking Pokémon*

Type: Normal
How to say it: LICK-i-tung
Height: 3' 11"
Weight: 144 lbs
Possible Moves: Lick, Wrap, Supersonic, Stomp, Disable, Defense Curl, Knock Off, Slam, Screech, Refresh
Does not evolve

KOFFING *Poison Gas Pokémon*

Type: Poison
How to say it: CAWF-ing
Height: 2' 0"
Weight: 2 lbs
Possible Moves: Posion Gas, Tackle, Smog, Sludge, Smokescreen, Selfdestruct, Haze, Explosion, Destiny Bond, Memento
Evolves: into Weezing

WEEZING *Poison Gas Pokémon*

Type: Poison
Pronunciation: WEEZE-ing
Height: 3' 11"
Weight: 21 lbs
Possible Moves: Poison Gas, Tackle, Smog, Sludge, Smokescreen, Selfdestruct, Haze, Explosion, Destiny Bond, Memento
Does not evolve

RHYHORN

Spikes Pokémon

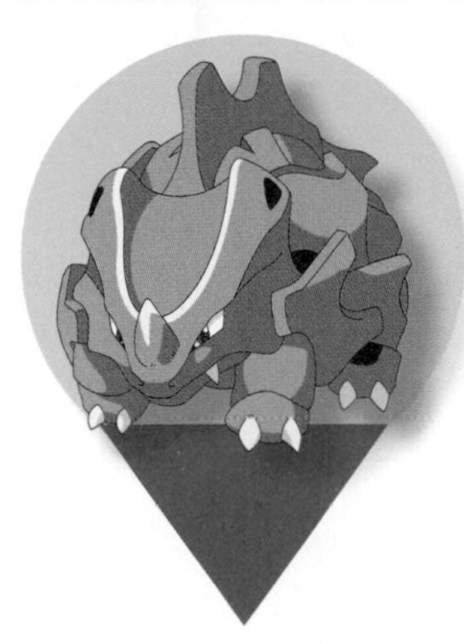

Type: Ground/Rock
How to say it: RYE-horn
Height: 3' 3"
Weight: 254 lbs
Possible Moves: Horn Attack, Tail Whip, Fury Attack, Scary Face, Rock Blast, Horn Drill, Take Down, Earthquake, Megahorn
Evolves: into Rhydon

RHYDON

Drill Pokémon

Type: Ground/Rock
How to say it: RYE-don
Height: 6' 3"
Weight: 265 lbs
Possible Moves: Horn Attack, Stomp, Tail Whip, Fury Attack, Scary Face, Rock Blast, Horn Drill, Leer, Take Down, Earthquake, Megahorn
Does not evolve

If your Pokémon gets run over by a Rhyhorn, visit Poké Mart for a potion or two!

If you see Rhyhorn charging at you, get out of the way, quick! This sturdy Pokémon will plow ahead, not caring what it smashes into. When it evolves into Rhydon, its armor becomes super thick. It can live in super hot lava with-out even feeling it!

Sweet and kindhearted Chansey loves to help injured Pokémon. This is why so many Chanseys work at Pokémon Centers.

CHANSEY *Egg Pokémon*

Type: Normal
How to say it: CHAN-see
Height: 3' 7"
Weight: 76 lbs
Possible Moves: Pound, Doubleslap, Sing, Growl, Tail Whip, Refresh, Softboiled, Minimize, Defense Curl, Light Screen, Double-Edge, Sing, Egg Bomb
Evolves: into Blissey with Friendship

BLISSEY *Happiness Pokémon*

Type: Normal
How to say it: BLISS-ie
Height: 4' 11"
Weight: 103 lbs
Possible Moves: Pound, Growl, Tail Whip, Refresh, Softboiled, Doubleslap, Minimize, Sing, Egg Bomb, Defense Curl, Light Screen, Double-Edge
Does not evolve

TANGELA *Vine Pokémon*

Type: Grass
How to say it: TANG-guh-luh
Height: 3' 3"
Weight: 77 lbs
Possible Moves: Ingrain, Constrict, Absorb, Poisonpowder, Vine Whip, Bind, Mega Drain, Stun Spore, Sleep Powder, Slam, Growth, Tickle
Does not evolve

KANGASKHAN *Parent Pokémon*

Type: Normal
How to say it: KANG-gus-con
Height: 7' 3"
Weight: 176 lbs
Possible Moves: Comet Punch, Rage, Bite, Tail Whip, Mega Punch, Leer, Dizzy Punch, Fake Out, Endure, Reversal
Does not evolve

Tangela's body is covered with vines. If one snaps off, a new one will grow back the very next day!

Kangaskhan carries its young in the pouch on its stomach. It is fiercely protective of its children.

If Horsea senses danger, it will shoot out water or ink from its mouth. Seadra uses its fins to protect itself. They have poison barbs, and Seadra can use them to swim backward if it needs to! And Kingdra has a special power. It can cause strong ocean currents—just by yawning!

HORSEA

Dragon Pokémon

Type: Water
How to say it: HORSE-ee
Height: 1' 4"
Weight: 18 lbs
Possible Moves: Bubble, Smokescreen, Leer, Water Gun, Twister, Agility, Hydro Pump, Dragon Dance
Evolves: into Seadra

SEADRA

Dragon Pokémon

Type: Water
How to say it: SEE-druh
Height: 3' 11"
Weight: 55 lbs
Possible Moves: Bubble, Smokescreen, Leer, Water Gun, Twister, Agility, Hydro Pump, Dragon Dance
Evolves: into Kingdra

KINGDRA

Dragon Pokémon

Type: Water/Dragon
How to say it: KING-druh
Height: 5' 11"
Weight: 335 lbs
Possible Moves: Bubble, Leer, Smokescreen, Water Gun, Twister, Agility, Hydro Pump, Dragon Dance
Does not evolve

GOLDEEN

Goldfish Pokémon

Type: Water
How to say it: GOAL-deen
Height: 2' 3"
Weight: 33 lbs
Possible Moves: Peck, Tail Whip, Water Sport, Supersonic, Horn Attack, Flail, Fury Attack, Waterfall, Horn Drill, Agility, Megahorn
Evolves: into Seaking

SEAKING

Goldfish Pokémon

Type: Water
How to say it: SEE-king
Height: 4' 3"
Weight: 86 lbs
Possible Moves: Peck, Tail Whip, Water Sport, Supersonic, Horn Attack, Flail, Fury Attack, Waterfall, Horn Drill, Agility, Megahorn
Does not evolve

Goldeen is nicknamed the Water Queen because its beautiful fins billow elegantly as it swims. Seaking is quite a sight, too. In autumn, large groups of them swim up streams and rivers, coloring the waters a brilliant red.

Ash's friend Misty likes to battle with these Poké-mon, probably because of their powerful Water Attacks. Both Staryu and Starmie have mysteri-ous, glowing cores.

STARYU

Star Shape Pokémon

Type: Water
How to say it: STAR-you
Height: 2' 7"
Weight: 76 lbs
Possible Moves: Tackle, Water Gun, Harden, Rapid Spin, Recover, Camouflage, Swift, Bubble-beam Minimize, Light Screen, Cosmic Power, Hydro Pump
Evolves: into Starmie with a Water Stone

STARMIE

Mysterious Pokémon

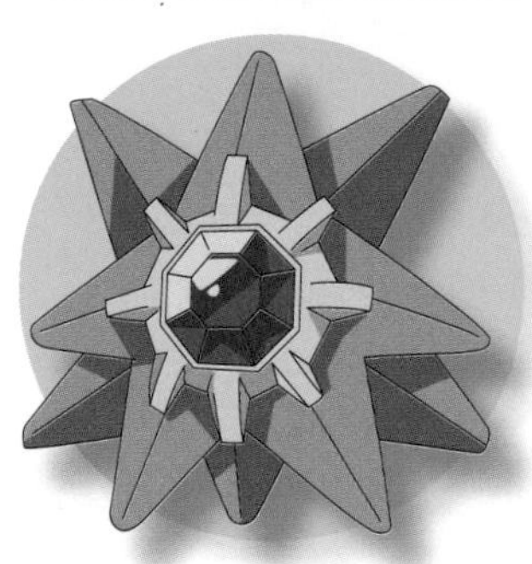

Type: Water/Psychic
How to say it: STAR-me
Height: 3' 7"
Weight: 176 lbs
Possible Moves: Water Gun, Rapid Spin, Recover, Swift, Confuse Ray
Does not evolve

MR. MIME
Barrier Pokémon

Type: Psychic
How to say it: MIS-ter mime
Height: 4' 3"
Weight: 120 lbs
Possible Moves: Confusion, Barrier, Light Screen, Doubleslap, Meditate, Substitute, Reflect, Magical Leaf, Encore, Psybeam, Recycle, Trick, Role Play, Psychic, Baton Pass, Safeguard
Does not evolve

SCYTHER
Mantis Pokémon

Type: Bug/Flying
How to say it: SYE-ther
Height: 4' 11"
Weight: 123 lbs
Possible Moves: Leer, Quick Attack, Pursuit, False Swipe, Wing Attack, Focus Energy, Double Team, Slash, Swords Dance, Agility, Fury Cutter
Evolves: into Scizor

SCIZOR
Scissors Pokémon

Type: Bug/Steel
How to say it: SYE-zor
Height: 5' 11"
Weight: 260 lbs
Possible Moves: Quick Attack, Leer, Focus Energy, Pursuit, False Swipe, Agility, Metal Claw, Slash, Swords Dance, Iron Defense, Fury Cutter
Does not evolve

Mr. Mime's pantomime act is more than just for fun. It uses the power in its fingers to turn the air around it into an invisible wall!

—

Scyther moves so fast in the grass, it's almost impossible to see. Then, watch out! It will swipe out, ninja-style, with its razor-edged wings. Scizor has patterns on its pincers that look like eyes. They make its opponents think it has three heads!

When Jynx walks, it looks like this Pokémon is dancing. If Jynx passes by a group of people, they'll start dancing without even realizing it.

SMOOCHUM

Kiss Pokémon

Type: Ice/Psychic
How to say it: SMOOCH-um
Height: 1' 4"
Weight: 14 lbs
Possible Moves: Confusion, Sing, Mean Look, Fake Tears, Psychic, Perish Song, Blizzard
Evolves: into Jynx

JYNX

Human Shape Pokémon

Type: Ice/Psychic
How to say it: JINCKS
Height: 4' 7"
Weight: 90 lbs
Possible Moves: Pound, Lick, Lovely Kiss, Powder Snow, Sing, Doubleslap, Ice Punch, Mean Look, Fake Tears, Body Slam, Perish Song, Blizzard
Does not evolve

ELEKID *Electric Pokémon*

Type: Electric
How to say it: EL-uh-kid
Height: 2' 0"
Weight: 52 lbs
Possible moves: Quick Attack, Leer, Thunderpunch, Light Screen, Swift, Screech, Thunderbolt, Thunder
Evolves: into Electabuzz

ELECTABUZZ *Electric Pokémon*

Type: Electric
How to say it: ee-LECK-tuh-buzz
Height: 3' 7"
Weight: 66 lbs
Possible moves: Quick Attack, Leer, Thunderpunch, Light Screen, Swift, Screech, Thunderbolt, Thunder
Does not evolve

Elekid stores electricity in its body. It rotates its arms to generate energy. Electabuzz likes to eat electricity generated by power plants. That's shocking!

Magmar are born in active volcanoes, and their bodies are always glowing with fire. You won't find Magby in the wild, but you can get one if you breed two Magmar.

MAGBY

Live Coal Pokémon

Type: Fire
How to say it: MAG-bee
Height: 2' 4"
Weight: 47 lbs
Possible moves: Ember, Leer, Smog, Fire Punch, Smokescreen, Sunny Day, Flamethrower, Confuse Ray, Fire Blast
Evolves: into Magmar

MAGMAR

Spitfire Pokémon

Type: Fire
How to say it: MAG-mar
Height: 4' 3"
Weight: 98 lbs
Possible moves: Ember, Leer, Confuse Ray, Fire Punch, Smokescreen, Smog, Flamethrower, Sunny Day, Fire Blast
Does not evolve

PINSIR

Stag Beetle Pokémon

Type: Bug
How to say it: PIN-sir
Height: 4' 1"
Weight: 121 lbs
Possible moves: Vicegrip, Seismic Toss, Bend, Revenge, Brick Break, Submission, Guillotine, Focus Energy, Harden, Swords Dance
Does not evolve

TAUROS

Wild Bull Pokémon

Type: Normal
How to say it: TOR-ose
Height: 4' 7"
Weight: 195 lbs
Possible Moves: Tackle, Tail Whip, Leer, Rage, Take Down, Horn Attack, Scary Face, Pursuit, Swagger, Rest, Thrash
Does not evolve

Pinsir is one big, strong, bug! It can lift an opponent twice its size with its horns and toss it to the ground.

Tauros live in herds. They are constantly fighting with each other to prove their strength.

Magikarp is not much use in battle. But if you catch one, don't give up on it. With enough training, it will evolve into mighty Gyarados! Now that's worth waiting for.

MAGIKARP

Fish Pokémon

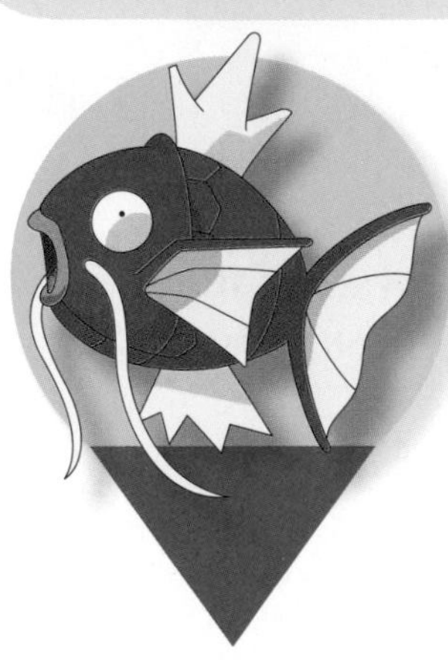

Type: Water
How to say it: MAJ-i-karp
Height: 2' 11"
Weight: 22 lbs
Possible Moves: Splash, Tackle, Flail
Evolves: into Gyarados

GYARADOS

Atrocious Pokémon

Type: Water/Flying
How to say it: GAR-i-dose
Height: 21' 4"
Weight: 518 lbs
Possible Moves: Thrash, Bite, Dragon Rage, Leer, Twister, Hydro Pump, Rain Dance, Dragon Dance, Hyper Beam
Does not evolve

LAPRAS

Transport Pokémon

Type: Water/Ice
How to say it: LAP-russ
Height: 8' 2"
Weight: 485 lbs
Possible Moves: Water Gun, Growl, Sing, Mist, Body Slam, Confuse Ray, Perish Song, Rain Dance, Safeguard, Ice Beam, Hydro Pump, Sheer Cold
Does not evolve

DITTO

Transform Pokémon

Type: Normal
How to say it: DID-oh
Height: 1' 0"
Weight: 9 lbs
Possible Moves: Transform
Does not evolve

Poor Lapras! This gentle Pokémon loves to give humans rides on its back, but it has been hunted almost to extinction.

The amazing Ditto can make itself look like any Pokémon it wants to by changing its cell structure. If you can make Ditto laugh while it is transformed, it will turn back to its original shape.

Eevee is a very unique little Pokémon. It can evolve into five different Types depending on what elemental stone it is exposed to. So what will it be? Vaporeon, which can control water? Electrically-charged Jolteon? Super hot Flareon? Espeon, with its mysterious psychic powers? Or a frightening Umbreon? The choice is up to you.

EEVEE

Evolution Pokémon

Type: Normal
How to say it: EE-vee
Height: 1' 0"
Weight: 14 lbs
Possible Moves: Tackle Sand-Attack, Quick Attack, Tail Whip, Bite, Take Down
Evolves: into Vaporeon with a Water Stone, into Jolteon with a Thunder Stone, into Flareon with a Fire Stone, into Espeon with Friendship during the day, and into Umbreon with Friendship at night

VAPOREON

Bubble Jet Pokémon

Type: Water
How to say it: vay-POR-ee-on
Height: 3' 3"
Weight: 64 lbs
Possible Moves: Aurora Beam, Tackle, Sand-Attack, Quick Attack, Water Gun, Tail Whip, Bite, Acid Armor, Haze, Helping Hand, Hydro Pump
Does not evolve

JOLTEON

Lightning Pokémon

Type: Electric
How to say it: JOLT-ee-on
Height: 2' 7"
Weight: 54 lbs
Possible moves: Tackle, Sand-Attack, Quick Attack, Thundershock, Tail Whip, Thunder Wave, Double Kick, Agility, Pin Missile, Thunder, Helping Hand
Does not evolve

FLAREON

Flame Pokémon

Type: Fire
How to say it: FLARE-ae-on
Height: 2' 1"
Weight: 55 lbs
Possible moves: Tackle, Sand-Attack, Quick Attack, Ember, Tail Whip, Bite, Leer, Fire Spin, Flamethrower, Helping Hand, Smog
Does not evolve

ESPEON

Sun Pokémon

Type: Psychic
How to say it: ESS-pee-on
Height: 2' 11"
Weight: 58 lbs
Possible Moves: Tackle, Tail Whip, Helping Hand, Sand-Attack, Confusion, Quick Attack, Swift, Psybeam, Psychic, Morning Sun
Does not evolve

UMBREON

Moonlight Pokémon

Type: Dark
How to say it: UMM-bree-on
Height: 3' 3"
Weight: 60 lbs
Possible Moves: Tackle, Tail Whip, Helping Hand, Sand-Attack, Quick Attack, Pursuit, Confuse Ray, Faint Attack, Mean Look, Screech, Moonlight
Does not evolve

Porygon is a man-made Poké-mon. It is capable of per-forming only tasks that are in its program. Porygon2 is the updated version of Po-rygon. It was designed for space travel.

PORYGON

Virtual Pokémon

Type: Normal
How to say it: POR-eh-gon
Height: 2' 7"
Weight: 80 lbs
Possible Moves: Tackle, Sharpen, Conversion, Conver-sion 2, Lock-On, Recycle, Zap Cannon, Recover, Psybeam, Harden, Agility, Tri Attack
Evolves: into Porygon2

PORYGON2

Virtual Pokémon

Type: Normal
How to say it: POR-eh-gon-too
Height: 2' 0"
Weight: 72 lbs
Possible Moves: Tackle, Con-version, Conversion 2, Agility, Psybeam, Recover, Defense Curl, Lock-On, Tri Attack, Recy-cle, Zap Cannon
Does not evolve

OMANYTE *Spiral Pokémon*

Type: Rock/Water
How to say it: OHM-uh-nite
Height: 1' 4"
Weight: 17 lbs
Possible Moves: Constrict, Water Gun, Withdraw, Bite, Leer, Mud Shot, Protect, Tickle, Ancientpower, Hydro Pump
Evolves: into Omastar

OMASTAR *Spiral Pokémon*

Type: Rock/Water
How to say it: AHM-uh-star
Height: 3' 3"
Weight: 77 lbs
Possible Moves: Constrict, Water Gun, Withdraw, Bite, Mud Shot, Protect, Tickle, Ancientpower, Leer, Spike Cannon, Hydro Pump
Does not evolve

Omanyte and Omastar were both extinct for years, until scientists regenerated them from fossils.

Like Omanyte and Omastar, Kabuto and Kabutops were generated from fossils. You'll find Kabuto on the sea floor, where its eyes glow in the darkness. Kabutops is known for being a fast swimmer.

KABUTO

Shellfish Pokémon

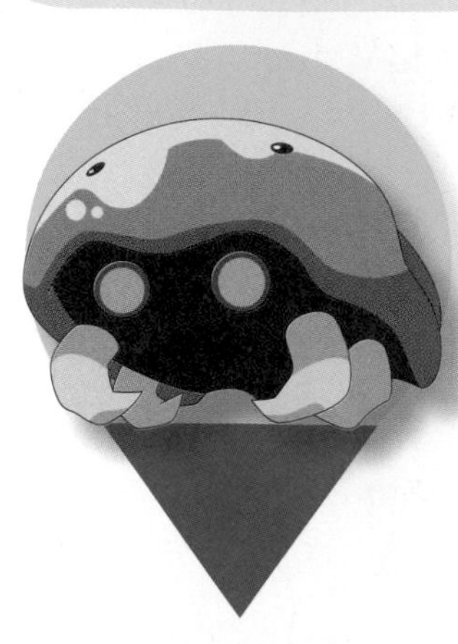

Type: Rock/Water
How to say it: kuh-BOO-toe
Height: 1' 8"
Weight: 25 lbs
Possible Moves: Scratch, Harden, Absorb, Slash, Mud Shot, Leer, Sand-Attack, Endure, Metal Sound, Mega Drain, Ancientpower
Evolves: into Kabutops

KABUTOPS

Shellfish Pokémon

Type: Rock/Water
How to say it: kuh-BOO-tops
Height: 4' 3"
Weight: 89 lbs
Possible Moves: Fury Cutter, Scratch, Harden, Absorb, Slash, Leer, Mud Shot, Sand-Attack, Endure, Metal Sound, Mega Drain, Ancientpower
Does not evolve

AERODACTYL *Fossil Pokémon*

Type: Rock/Flying
How to say it: air-oh-DACK-tull
Height: 5' 11"
Weight: 130 lbs
Possible Moves: Wing Attack, Agility, Supersonic, Bite, Ancient-power, Scary Face, Take Down, Hyper Beam
Does not evolve

SNORLAX *Sleeping Pokémon*

Type: Normal
How to say it: SNORE-lacks
Height: 6' 11"
Weight: 1014 lbs
Possible Moves: Tackle, Defense Curl, Belly Drum, Headbutt, Yawn, Snore, Sleep Talk, Block, Covet, Rollout, Amnesia, Rest, Body Slam, Hyper Beam
Does not evolve

Scientists say that ferocious Aerodactyl flew through the skies during the age of dinosaurs. It was regenerated from some DNA found in amber.

Snorlax likes to sleep and eat all day long. This extra-large Pokémon is very lazy and will eat anything.

All three of these legendary Bird Pokémon possess amazing powers. Articuno can control ice and snow. When Zapdos flaps its wings, it creates lightning, and savage thunderstorms follow. And Moltres has flaming wings and can control fire.

ARTICUNO

Freeze Pokémon

Type: Ice/Flying
How to say it: are-ti-KOO-no
Height: 5' 7"
Weight: 122 lbs
Possible Moves: Gust, Powder Snow, Mind Reader, Ice Beam, Blizzard, Agility, Mist, Reflect, Sheer Cold
Does not evolve

ZAPDOS

Electric Pokémon

Type: Electric/Flying
How to say it: ZAP-dose
Height: 5' 3"
Weight: 116 lbs
Possible moves: Peck, Thundershock, Thunder Wave, Drill Peck, Charge, Thunder, Agility, Light Screen, Detect
Does not evolve

MOLTRES

Flame Pokémon

Type: Fire/Flying
How to say it: MOLE-trace
Height: 6' 7"
Weight: 132 lbs
Possible Moves: Wing Attack, Ember, Fire Spin, Endure, Agility, Sky Attack, Flamethrower, Safeguard, Heat Wave
Does not evolve

DRATINI *Dragon Pokémon*

Type: Dragon
How to say it: druh-TEE-nee
Height: 5' 11"
Weight: 7 lbs
Possible Moves: Wrap, Leer, Twister, Thunder Wave, Agility, Slam, Dragon Rage, Safeguard, Outrage, Hyper Beam
Evolves: into Dragonair

DRAGONAIR *Dragon Pokémon*

Type: Dragon
How to say it: drag-uh-NAIR
Height: 13' 1"
Weight: 36 lbs
Possible Moves: Wrap, Leer, Thunder Wave, Twister, Safeguard, Outrage, Agility, Slam, Dragon Rage, Hyper Beam
Evolves: into Dragonite

DRAGONITE *Dragon Pokémon*

Type: Dragon/Flying
How to say it: Drag-uh-NITE
Height: 7' 3"
Weight: 463 lbs
Possible Moves: Wrap, Leer, Thunder Wave, Twister, Agility, Slam, Dragon Rage, Safeguard, Wing Attack, Outrage, Hyper Beam
Does not evolve

These Dragon Pokémon seem like something out of a fairy tale. Dratini constantly sheds its skin as it grows. When it evolves into Dragonair, it gains the ability to control the weather. And its final evolved form, Dragonite, is kind and as intelligent as a human.

Because Mew contains the genetic codes of every Poké-mon, it is thought to be the ancestor of all Pokémon. Scientists used DNA from Mew to create Mewtwo. Its purpose? To be the strongest Pokémon ever. To this day, Pokemon fans argue over which Poké-mon is harder to beat—Mewtwo or Mew.

MEWTWO
Genetic Pokémon

Type: Psychic
How to say it: MYU-too
Height: 6' 7"
Weight: 269 lbs
Possible Moves: Confusion, Disable, Swift, Barrier, Psy-chic, Recover, Mist, Safeguard, Amnesia, Psych Up, Future Sight
Does not evolve

MEW

New Species Pokémon

Type: Psychic
How to say it: myu
Height: 1' 4"
Weight: 9 lbs
Possible Moves: unknown
Does not evolve

Ash saw Mewtwo and Mew battle once. The fight ended in a tie!

INDEX

INDEX

NOTES